City M

CITY MUSIC

Elaine Feinstein

HUTCHINSON
London Sydney Auckland Johannesburg

This edition first published in 1990 by
Hutchinson

Century Hutchinson Ltd, Random Century House,
20 Vauxhall Bridge Road, London SW1V 2SA

Century Hutchinson Australia (Pty) Ltd
20 Alfred Street, Milsons Point, Sydney, NSW 2061,
Australia

Century Hutchinson New Zealand Limited
PO Box 40–086, Glenfield, Auckland 10, New Zealand

Century Hutchinson South Africa (Pty) Ltd
PO Box 337, Bergvlei, 2012 South Africa

British Library Cataloguing in Publication Data
Feinstein, Elaine, *1930–*
    City music
    I. Title
    821.914

    ISBN 0-09-174317-6

Set in Times by 🅰 Tek Art Ltd, Croydon, Surrey
Printed and bound in Great Britain by Cox & Wyman

For Tony Whittome

Some of these poems first appeared in the *TLS, The Sunday Times* and *The Poetry Book Society Anthology*. The Lyrics of Nika Turbina first appeared in *First Draft, Poems of Nika Turbina* (Marion Boyars, London, New York). Literal versions were made by Antonina Bouis.

Contents

PART ONE

CITY MUSIC

Urban Lyric

The gaunt lady of the service wash
stands on the threshold and blinks in the sunlight.

Her face is yellow in its frizz of hair
and yet she smiles as if she were fortunate.

She listens to the hum of cars passing
as if she were on a country lane in summer,

or as if the tall trees edging this
busy street scattered blessings on her.

Last month they cut a cancer out of her throat.
This morning she tastes sunshine in the dusty air.

And she is made alert to the day's beauty,
as if her terror had wakened poetry.

Annus Mirabilis 1989

Ten years ago, beneath the Hotel Astoria,
   we watched a dissident cabaret in Budapest,
where they showed Einstein as a Jewish tailor.
   All the women on stage were elegantly dressed.

Their silken garments were cleverly slit to expose
   illicit glimpses of delicate thighs and breast.
Einstein was covered with chalk, in ill-fitting clothes;
   he was taking measurements, trying to please the rest.

At the climax of the play, to applause and laughter
   they raked him with strobe lights and the noise of guns.
I was chilled by the audience euphoria.
   Of course, I don't have a word of Hungarian,

and afterwards there were embarrassed explanations,
   which left out tailoring and obsequious gestures.
Their indignation was all about nuclear science, while
   I pondered the resilience of an old monster.

Infidelities

Last night she ran out barefoot over
the wet gravel to call him back
from the street. This morning,
in the tranquillity of bath water,

she wonders when it was she first shivered
with the wish for more than ordinary happiness.
How did she fall in love with poetry
that clear eyed girl she was?

Late at night, by a one-bar heater,
her unpainted lips parted
on the words of dead poets.
She was safer in the dance hall.

'And if you can't love poetry,'
she muses. 'What was there of me
all those years ago, apart from
that life of which it is made?

Only an inhospitable hostess,
a young woman in an old dress.'

A Favourite Uncle

In your Bing Crosby blazer, you were
handsome and clean, and smelled of lavender.

When I kept trying to kirby grip
my electric brown hair away from my face,

you showed me how to comb it loose.
My aunts dived like seals into the cold sea

on Southport sands. Your gentle grip checked me
in salty wind to have me listen to

a scratch string band, and steered
my bony elbow with a courteous gesture.

At ninety now you use that same pressure
crossing your Bootle street, and I feel again

like a child that could rely on male protection.
I can't, because I have not lived as I should,

and you need my help these days, being confused
by a town, you say, is always being moved

around your tall Victorian house that stands
anomalous among the shopping malls.

Convalescence

These yellow afternoons, dark skies, wet streets.
Only the harshest taste reaches through to me.
Nothing I read bites in. My Jules Verne
window seat noses a sunken world
of willows dragging in muggy air and
flowers drowning in mud, skidding
a bridged river, skips of rubble,
dead osiers. The days run under me.
Tock.   Tock.
I count them. Even as I feel
beneath my nightgown quietly
flesh pinched together like dough
begin to crust and heal.

Going Back to Cambridge

There they all are on the lawn
in warm air sweet as milk
eating strawberries on the grass.

I remember them awkward and young:
the men with scuffed leather elbows,
the women carelessly dressed.

The men are in dark suits now;
they have Chairs, they are part of
The Royal Society's Fellowship,

one has been knighted, yet I wonder if
any of our adolescent selves
would have been delighted

to see how far we have moved from that shabby
city of leaky gas fires and broken lino
which so bewitched our spirits long ago.

Childhood Tyranny

It must have been 3 am when she said to me
'No point in going to sleep.

As soon as we drop off, that alarm
will ring and it'll be time for school.'

I was so tired, I couldn't even reply
but my body wouldn't be pinched awake:

for my forensic skill poor evidence.
The body wisely has its own defence.

Photographs

At twelve I didn't like my own face, because
my eyes were huge and open as a dog's,
and I wanted slitty eyes like Virginia Mayo.

Photographs show me laughing and healthy,
with wide shoulders and strong wrists that could take me
up the pear tree to the highest boughs.

Between these brown card covers adolescence
stirs. 'Oh Daddy,' I asked once
'why aren't I prettier?' He was kindly but embarrassed.

Now I look back on photographs of that girl
as if I were already some ginger haired ghost
visiting a sepia world of strangers,

and among so many faces I like most
her laughter lines, strong nose and windblown hair.
And if I could fly back I should whisper to her

where she stands, painted and scared in the dance hall
setting out her sexual wares: What you
think of as disadvantages will bring you through.

Hayfever

When Timothy grass and Rye pollen flew
each year, I began to honk like a goose.

It was always summer and party time
for kissing and rolling in the grass

so I couldn't bear to stay at home in bed.
I painted my face with beige pancake

put drops in my eyes, and learnt instead
as my membranes flared and I gasped for air

how to feel out of things
even when there.

Valentine for a Middle-aged Spouse

Dear Love, since we might both be dead by now
through war, disease, hijack or accident
at least for one day let's not speak of how
much we have bickered, botched and badly spent.
Wouldn't it make much more sense to collude
in an affectionate work of camouflage,
turning our eyes away from all we've skewed,
to the small gains of household bricolage?
As our teeth loosen and our faces crag
(I shall grow skinnier as you grow paunched,
a Laurel to your Hardy, not much brag),
I'll think of all our love most sweetly launched
if you will look with favour on these lines
we may still live as tender valentines.

Homecoming

The light is sullen today, yet people are
bustling in the rainy street under my window,

poking in the Cypriot grocers for aubergines,
buying their strings of garlic and onions;

they can choose between the many seeds on
the bread: rye, sesame, cumin.

Across the road, the pharmacy windows
are lettered in brass like a Victorian shop.

In the coffee house with its heavy green and gold
pottery, they serve bean soup with sausages

and the accents of old Vienna mingle
with California. In the countryside

every one of us would be found peculiar.
We'd leak away. In Englands Lane

(through road for taxis and the Camden hoppa)
this city music and a few friends keep me sane.

Snowy Landscapes

Yesterday, I flew in over the landscape
my grandfather tried to farm near Montreal.
There was ice in the stubble, hard snow,
and flat spaces that made me flinch
to imagine the winter below.

Now in mountain country in Colorado
the snow's whiteness has us catching our breath,
rejoicing at the violence of sunlight here;
and even at night when so many storms gather
enjoying the flash on the snow.

Why do mountains soothe us? They should alarm.
Instead, their snows seem to induce in us
a queer spirit of compassionate calm:
as if their beauty lit our thought so sharply
we become equal to the threat of harm.

Getting Older

The first surprise: I like it.
Whatever happens now, some things
that used to terrify have not:

I didn't die young, for instance. Or lose
my only love. My three children
never had to run away from anyone.

Don't tell me this gratitude is complacent.
We all approach the edge of the same blackness
which for me is silent.

Knowing as much sharpens
my delight in January freesia,
hot coffee, winter sunlight. So we say

as we lie close on some gentle occasion:
every day won from such
darkness is a celebration.

Aviation

Tonight our bodies lie unused like clothes flung
  over a bed. I can taste brown rain.
Flat land, wet land, I can feel your winter
  seeping into my blood like an old sickness.
This is your season of waiting and warm convalescence
  when restful spirits can be quiet and gentle.
Why am I feverish then, what are these
  troubled insomniac beckonings?
What are they to me, the islands where
  falcons breed, or green rivers
where red mullet and shad swim up from the sea?

I have a monster in my head, yellow
  and surly as a camel, an old woman
clutching a hot bottle against the damp,
  and I recognise her face. She frightens me,
more than the loneliness of being awake in the dark.
  And so I put on skinny leather wings and my
home-made cage of basket wear and start
  my crazy flapping run. In this light
I must look like an old enthusiast in
  daguerreotype. These marshlands
clog the feet. I know, but then
  I may not rise, but all night long I run.

Debts to Marina Tsvetayeva

Tough as canvas, Marina, your soul
was stretched out once against the gale
and now your words have become sails.
You travel far into a darkness
I don't plead for since I can't aspire
to join your spirit on that Christian
star whose fire is green and cool
in your imagination of heaven.

Mothers, Marina, yours and mine, would
have recognised a bleak and dutiful spirit
in each other: we were supposed to
conquer the worlds they had renounced.
Instead, we served poetry, neither of us
prepared either for marriage or the solitary life.
Yours was the lyric voice of abandon
only sobered by poverty and homesickness.
Once or twice I felt the same loneliness,

but I can never learn from you, Marina,
since poetry is always a question of language,
though I have often turned to you in thought as if
your certainties could teach me how to bear
the littleness of what we are on our own
without books, or music, or even a pen;
or as if your stern assurance of the spirit
could preserve us on that ocean we sail alone.

Blasphemy Laws

Today the plump flesh of a white crocus
has broken through the dry earth at the tube station,

and the dusty hedges on Haverstock Hill
have begun to put out pale new leaf.

Their ungardened roots are responding
to an inner code and the motion of the planet

both forces clearly independent of us.
Doesn't a law to protect God seem blasphemous?

Blue Snow

A winter evening, I recall,
on quiet streets, a young girl
running in broken shoes

over the snow. She goes
hurrying to a lover,
to heal their quarrel.

Her hot face is wet
with a fever of 102°.
Next week, in the hospital,

she whispers again and again:
'your lips are salt' and
'the snow is blue.'

Circe's Island

Circe, he called me, as if
he had thrown away the onward
movement of his life

to lie within my arms, as if
my inner dream had
damaged him.

Is it possible? I thought to be
Penelope weaving stories
to furnish a cold house.

I argue, Circe was wronged.
She did not poison but enchant
spirits of those who lost their way.

I claim no drug persuaded
Odysseus to take his ease
so long beneath her sweet spice trees.

But I know myths are dangerous.
All the harm is done,
and these ten years are gone.

And how can I console him,
my broken-hearted prince,
for his lost kingdom?

Muse

for E.T.

'Write something every day,' she said,
'even if it's only a line,
it will protect you.'

How should this be?
Poetry opens no cell,
heals no hurt body,

brings back no lover,
altogether, poetry is
powerless as grass.

How then should it defend us?
unless by strengthening
our fierce and obstinate centres.

Dignity

An old poet has come to the Festival,
his books lie over the table, we all

marvel at him. He is already sure
of his place in the history of literature.

I watch his weariness, the way
his eyes flicker without envy

over the students with everything still to do.
Against probabilities, I should like to

believe in the perfection of his life
yet I observe: he has a young wife.

PART TWO

EIGHT SONGS FROM 'THE BET'

An opera for puppets

The Puppet Opera, 'The Bet', was first performed
at the Purcell Room in July 1990, and went on
to the Almeida Theatre in the same month.

Argument

When the son of an old widow leaves home to seek
his fortune, she gives him a ring and makes him
promise not to part with it. After he's gone,
a wandering Spirit of Unhappiness visits the widow.
The Spirit makes a bet with the widow that her son can
be persuaded to part with the ring. If the widow
wins she may have anything she desires. If she
loses she must give up her hope. The Spirit adopts
several disguises and tries to tempt the boy to part
with the ring, first through fear, then through greed,
and at last through love.

The Widow's Song

I used to enjoy being quiet and alone,
Making jam, or choosing colours for my weaving,
Potting hares, or baking roots, I always hummed a song,
And I never had the time for grieving.
But now there's no one needing my attention,
It's as much as I can do to keep
The larder clean, and sweep . . .

Look at the soup that's on the table.
The pan it comes from stands completely empty.
There isn't one last drop left on the ladle.
I promise you there's nothing in the pantry.
There's nothing in this hut.
No food left and no wood.
How can I make a bet?
I've no food for the morning,
And no goods to sell.
How can I make a bet?

The Ring

Here is a ring that isn't worth much money.
I've never been entirely sure it's silver.
The stone is malachite, which may be lucky
So take it now and put it on your finger.
Remember just one thing –
Don't give away the ring!

Think of it as a sign of my affection
Your father, whom I loved, gave it to me.
I always thought of his love as protection.
While you are gone, I'll pray for your safe journey.
Just promise me one thing,
Don't give away the ring.

Song of the Spirit of Unhappiness

Look at how delicate and frail I am!
In my large eyes are pools of need.
How much I need, how little I expect to have.
I draw the life from everyone I meet.

Look at the darkness in my dangerous eyes,
And see the longing of my empty soul.
I'm looking for a treasure I will recognise,
When it makes my poor unhappy spirit whole.

What the Spirit of Unhappiness Wants

Hope cheers the farmer when the sky is red.
Hope saves the lost man when the moors are misty.
Hope gets the poor man out of bed
And keeps him going when the days are grisly.

And what you have is Hope in real abundance.
You wake with Hope each morning, like a miracle.
Whatever else, your hand has never lost that thread.
What you have that I don't is Hope . . . it's simple!

Song of the Forest

He's made a fire to warm him
And dreams of childhood play,
Of snowballs and toboggans,
Hot pies and happy days.

Nothing now disturbs his rest.
No fear of the dark place.
Cold moonlight in the forest,
Hardly reaches his young face.

Painted City Song

The shop windows of the city glitter daily
With pairs of satin shoes on heels like spiders,
Gold capes, and veils of silver lace, and jewels.
Rich people in their furs survey them grandly.
And for what it cost to buy a pair of curtains,
You could live for two good years in the mountains.

Work Song

Knock, knock. I've got strong muscles.
With heart and muscle, I'll work so hard.
All that I need is a chance to prove my willingness!
I'll settle for a kennel in your cold back yard.

Richest Woman's Song

I can live on lark's tongues
Snails in butter, caviare . . .
I can eat with silver spoons
And sleep beneath a lion's fur,
But still I need somebody, young and supple,
To work for me with all his heart and muscle.

PART THREE

TEN LYRICS of Nika Turbina

from the Russian

We speak a different language,
you and I.
The script may be the same,
but the words are strange.
You and I
live on different
islands, even though
we are in the same apartment.

1983

Long Distance Calls

Long distance calls
are in a race with God
all around the planet –
who can win it?
Your noise breaks through the glass
between the Lord and me.
I'm finished with such calls,
finished with calls!

I'll speak to Him in silence
(only our eyes meeting)
of how to save the earth
that is so sick of shouting.
And as the grass is rustled,
and leaves swirl in the wind
over my wounded earth,
we will speak in silence
of how not
to kill childhood.

1983

Rain, night, a broken window
and shards of glass
stuck up in the air
like leaves the wind does not pick up.

Suddenly, there is a sound of ringing . . .
That is exactly how
a human life breaks off.

1981

I Will Clean the House

I will clean the house
and put the furniture
in empty corners.
I will wash the floor
and fix the rugs,
and then sit down.
Behind the window panes
the rain will splash
and the day will punish me
with horrible loneliness.
I want so much
to go around the gate
and into the garden,
so I can look at all the flowers there.
But every morning instead
I start the day dusting,
and shutting the windows
against the wind.

1983

Where are you living now
invisible soul?
Your tiny home
must be lovely.
You are wandering
alone in the city
invisible soul
and I can't see you.

1983

Remembrance

I want to sit alone with you
I want to sit alone
near the old house,
the house that stands
by the river of memory.
The print of your bare foot
smells of last summer's sun,
where you and I wandered
on the still unmown grass.
The skies were blue,
and disappeared beyond the outskirts.
Voices rang out
and that's all I remember.
The accounting of the days
has reached an end.
Like a flock of birds
all the days
have gathered at our feet.
I don't know what to feed them,
there are no lines left.

1981

Three Oranges

I'll bring home
three oranges in
a blue handkerchief.
There are city smells of
gas and cold,
and I blow on my fingers,
but suddenly
there are three oranges on the street
like a circle of sun.
Feet, wheels,
sledges in the slush . . .
What I see are three oranges
burning in a blue handkerchief

and the sky and the garden.

1983

I Want Kindness

How often
I catch sidelong glances
and sharp words hurt me
like arrows
I implore you – listen! You must not
destroy the shortlived
childlike dreams in me.
My day is so small,
and I want kindness
so much
for everyone
even those
who aim
at me.

1983

Sing me a lullaby, rock me
to sleep, cover me with a blanket:
deceive me with your lulling,
give me your dreams in the morning.

On some days the image of
the sun is bluer than ice,
put that under my pillow
in the morning, but don't wait.

Listen, don't wait.
Childhood has run away from me.

1982

As my lashes close, the day ends
but I can't sleep.
I think about the passing day
which has gone by without
reaching the night,
about streets exhausted by people
and streetlights, weary
with the effort of shining
and about this house in which I can't sleep,
until sleep, an anxious grey bird,
flies up to me suddenly
at daybreak.
Now wake up, little thing,
early in the morning
and you'll see how
your streetlight has been resting,
laughter has filled the crossroads,
and a long time has gone by since evening.

1981

PART FOUR

BALLADS FROM 'THE TEMPTATION OF WILLIAM FOSTERS'

A radio play with music

In Praise of Gift Horses

Some people treat my best gifts with suspicion
Some fears are learnt as early as the font.
You think the Devil's just a superstition
yet still go on refusing what you want.

Let's say . . .
Some fellow finds himself
back in the slammer
and some nark suggests
a way he can be free:
he'd be well advised to take
the chance and stammer:
'Yes, I'd like to be outside
in the sunshine with my bride,'
and not look sourly at the offered key.

Let's say . . .
You find some massive
banking error
leaves your overdraft
some thousands to the good.
No one is hurt by that,
so where's the terror?
Surely any family man
will take a fortune when he can?
Don't hesitate, I say. Nobody should.

It's true that long ago . . .
there was some hanky-panky
in a shower of heavenly gold.
And if the Trojans hadn't pulled
that horse in, Ulysses'

plan would have been foiled.
But you must see all that makes
those acts immoral are – mistakes!
Fear the disaster, not the offer, frankly.

So don't treat all my best gifts with suspicion
forget the fears you took on at the font.
Morality is only superstition.
So why go on refusing what you want?

Ballad of Surprising Turnups

It's something people have to learn . . .
Since nothing in this world of ours is certain,
You needn't treat the future with respect.
You really can't predict what's going to happen,
by using laws of cause and their effect.
In this pursuit astrologers and journalists
waste all their words of wisdom and analysis.
They never know which way the coin will turn.

Walking by the Berlin Wall
a year ago, machine guns placed
where they could kill:
nobody thought, nobody guessed
that it would fall.
Now what comes next?
No one can tell.

A writer sat in prison then.
Committees worked to set him free
from his oppressive government:
nobody thought, nobody guessed,
he would become a President.
Now what comes next?
Let's wait and see.

And that black leader, held
in gaol for thirty years
to keep the peace:
Who would have thought
he'd be released?
And what comes next?
There's hopes and fears.

And those today, who
wash up cups
and take abuse
for all you know, for all you guess
may find some use
for energy,
which sets them free.

As William Fosters, trodden
down at work and home
is given a chance:
for the first time
of all he wants.
How will he be?
We're going to see.

It's something people have to learn . . .
Since nothing in this world of ours is certain,
You cannot treat the future with respect
You really can't predict what's going to happen,
by using laws of cause and their effect.
In this pursuit, astrologers and journalists
waste all their words of wisdom and analysis.
They never know which way the coin will turn.